DEFINING AND ACHIEVING DECISIVE VICTORY

D1798574

Colin S. Gray

April 2002

Preparation of this study was supported by the U.S. Army War College's Exernal Research Associates Program. For information see http://www.carlisle.army.mil/usassi/erap.pdf.

*****

Comments pertaining to this report are invited and should be forwarded to: Director, Strategic Studies Institute, U.S. Army War College, 122 Forbes Ave., Carlisle, PA 17013-5244. Copies of this report may be obtained from the Publications Office by calling (717) 245-4133, FAX (717) 245-3820, or via the Internet at Rita.Rummel@ carlisle.army.mil

*****

Most 1993, 1994, and all later Strategic Studies Institute (SSI) monographs are available on the SSI Homepage for electronic dissemination. SSI's Homepage address is: http://www.carlisle.army. mil/usassi/welcome.htm

*****

The Strategic Studies Institute publishes a monthly e-mail newsletter to update the national security community on the research of our analysts, recent and forthcoming publications, and upcoming conferences sponsored by the Institute. Each newsletter also provides a strategic commentary by one of our research analysts. If you are interested in receiving this newsletter, please let us know by e-mail at outreach@carlisle.army.mil or by calling (717) 245-3133.

ISBN 1-58487-089-3

FOREWORD

The United States was thrust so suddenly into the war on terrorism that it was forced to deal with both immediate operational issues and broad strategic questions simultaneously. Even while the American military is consolidating battlefield success in Afghanistan, strategic thinkers and leaders are developing a long-term strategy. In this process, nothing is more important than defining victory.

In this monograph, Dr. Colin Gray, one of the world's leading strategic thinkers, explores the concept of victory in the war in terrorism, but he does so by placing it within the larger currents of change that are sweeping the global security environment. He contends that the time-tested idea of decisive victory is still an important one, but must be designed very carefully in this dangerous new world. To do so correctly can provide the foundation for an effective strategy. To fail to do so could be the first step toward strategic defeat.

The Strategic Studies Institute is pleased to publish this study as a contribution to the defeat of global terrorism.

DOUGLAS C. LOVELACE, JR.
Director
Strategic Studies Institute

BIOGRAPHICAL SKETCH OF THE AUTHOR

COLIN S. GRAY is Professor of International Politics and Strategic Studies at the University of Reading, England. A graduate of the Universities of Manchester and Oxford, Dr. Gray worked at the International Institute for Strategic Studies (London), and at Hudson Institute (Croton-on-Hudson, NY), before founding a defense-oriented think-tank in the Washington area, the National Institute for Public Policy. Dr Gray served for 5 years in the Reagan administration on the President's General Advisory Committee on Arms Control and Disarmament. He has served as an adviser both to the U.S. and the British governments (he has dual citizenship). His government work has included studies of nuclear strategy, arms control policy, maritime strategy, space strategy, and the use of special forces. Dr. Gray has written 17 books, most recently *Modern Strategy* (1999). In 2002 he will publish *Strategy for Chaos: RMA Theory and the Evidence of History* and *Future Warfare*.

SUMMARY

The idea of victory, let alone decisive victory, was very much out of style during the Cold War. The theory and practice of limited war in the nuclear age was more concerned to minimize the risks of escalation to nuclear holocaust than to win the conflict of the day. That changed dramatically with the end of the Cold War; indeed so much so that from 1991 to the present, with the painful exception of Somalia, the United States has known nothing but victory in its exercise of military power. The author challenges the view that war lacks the power of decision, arguing instead that war, even when not concluding with clear success for one side, still has the power of decision. This monograph discusses the idea of decisive victory with reference to different levels of analysis—the operational, strategic, and political. It is suggested that the concept of decisive victory needs to be supplemented by two ancillary concepts, strategic success and strategic advantage.

The author explores the means and methods most conducive to achievement of decisive victory. He explains that objectively "better" armies tend to win (war may be the realm of chance, but the dice are loaded in favor of those who are militarily competent); that there is no magic formula which can guarantee victory (not even today's information-led revolution in military affairs [RMA], which tends to equate precise firepower with war); that technology is not a panacea, the answer to all military and strategy difficulties; that the complexity of war and strategy allows for innovative, even asymmetrical, exercises in substitution as belligerents strive to emphasize strength and conceal weakness; and that it is essential to know your enemies, especially if you require them to cooperate in a deterrent or coercive relationship.

The author concludes by arguing that the concept of decisive victory is meaningful and important. Also it advises that different enemies in different wars will require the application of different military means and methods. One size in military style will not fit all cases. Readers are recommended not to think of decisive victory in terms of a simple either/or. Strategic success or advantage may serve the goals of policy quite well enough. Finally, the point is made that, among Western states at least, the United States today is surely unique in being interested in the idea of and capability for decisive military victory. America's European allies currently do not discern any serious military issues as clouds on their peaceful horizons.

DEFINING AND ACHIEVING DECISIVE VICTORY

The political object—the original motive for the war—will thus determine both the military objective to be reached and the amount of effort required.

Carl von Clausewitz, 1832

To study a war without taking into account the circumstances in which it is fought and the peace to which it led is a kind of historical pornography.

Sir Michael Howard, 1999

In war there can be no substitute for victory.

General Douglas MacArthur, 1951.

Introduction.

The justification for this monograph was explained succinctly in a brilliant essay written a generation ago by French scholar, Raymond Aron. "Strategic thought draws its inspiration each century, or rather at each moment of history, from the problems which events themselves pose."[1] Since September 11, 2001, it has been open season for efforts to grapple with the deceptively simple concept of victory. Journalists and other commentators have penned analyses with such titles as "The elusive character of victory," and "What Victory Means."[2] If "victory" unadorned is hard to corral intellectually, what sense can we make of "decisive victory"? Is the concept a theoretical artifact from a past age, or does it retain vitality, particularly for the hegemonic United States of today? I will argue that decisive victory, adjective and noun, is a meaningful and important concept.

Before plunging into the muddy waters of definition, it may be useful to recall a little history. Although since 1991

1

victory has come back into fashion as a proper outcome to be expected of the use of American arms, for the duration of the Cold War it was most emphatically one of yesterday's ideas. In very good part for reason of the sensible fear of escalation to nuclear holocaust, the only kind of conflict that the United States dared wage in the nuclear era was limited war. Writing at the tail end of the golden decade of modern American strategic thought (1955-66), Thomas C. Schelling argued that

> "victory" inadequately expresses what a nation wants from its military forces. Mostly it wants, in these times, the influence that resides in latent force. It wants the bargaining power that comes from its capacity to hurt, not just the direct consequence of successful military action. Even total victory over an enemy provides at best an opportunity for unopposed violence against the enemy populations. How to use that opportunity in the national interest, or in some wider interest, can be just as important as the achievement of victory itself; but traditional military suicide does not tell us how to use that capacity for inflicting pain.[3]

To strategic sophisticates in the 1950s and 1960s, victory was an atavistic notion. American theorists found the Clausewitz that they wanted to find in *On War*, which is to say the post-1827 Clausewitz who revised some of his manuscript in order to balance his discussion of "absolute war" with consideration of "real war" for limited aims.[4] But on the first page of Book One, Chapter 1, Clausewitz insists that *"War is thus an act of force to compel our enemy to do our will."*[5] He rams the point home by saying that "to impose our will on the enemy is its object [the object of the act of force that is war]. To secure that object we must render the enemy powerless; and that, in theory, is the true aim of warfare." Of course, in the sentences quoted the great man is explaining and exploring the nature of war, not offering advice on its conduct. But Clausewitz's admirably terse summary of the nature and object of war did not find much intellectual favor in Cold War America. After all, in a nuclear age would it not be dangerous in the extreme, even perilously irresponsible,

2

to attempt "to compel our enemy to do our will"? Has not Michael Quinlan written persuasively that "a nuclear state is a state that no one can afford to make desperate."[6] To extend Quinlan's point, a nuclear state is a state against which no one can afford to press for victory.

Readers can imagine the shock and horror that resulted when in 1980 I published (with Keith B. Payne) an article on nuclear strategy bearing the exciting title, "Victory Is Possible."[7] A year earlier I had expounded at some length on "Nuclear Strategy: The Case for a Theory of Victory," but the pages of *International Security,* or my dense prose, probably were too forbidding to attract nonacademics.[8] While I was trying to inject a little strategic reasoning into debate over what passed for nuclear strategy, others made like complaint about extra-nuclear matters also. For example, in a characteristically robust essay of 1982 vintage entitled "On the Meaning of Victory," Edward N. Luttwak recorded his view that:

> The West has become comfortably habituated to defeat. Victory is viewed with great suspicion, if not outright hostility. After all, if the right-thinking are to achieve their great aim of abolishing war they must first persuade us that victory is futile or, better still, actually harmful.[9]

Through the middle years of the 1980s, and in good part to help offset the belligerent facade of earlier talk of the United States "prevailing" in a nuclear war,[10] Secretary of Defense Casper Weinberger repeated the sensible sounding mantra that "a nuclear war cannot be won and must never be fought."[11] He had earlier aired the following thought, which, despite its honesty and common-sense logic, had not played too well politically: "You show me a Secretary of Defense who's planning not to prevail, and I'll show you a Secretary of Defense who ought to be impeached."[12]

Luttwak's 1982 judgment that "[v]ictory is viewed with great suspicion, if not outright hostility," was to be vindicated on the grand scale a decade later, when most Western scholars of the subject insisted that although the

Union of Soviet Socialist Republics (USSR) lost the Cold War, the United States had not won it.[13] So far out of strategic fashion had victory become, that the decade 1991-2001 should have caused some traumatic shock among professional pessimists. With the exception of the Somalia debacle of 1993-94, the United States enjoyed a decade of all but unalloyed strategic success. From the Gulf War in 1991, through Bosnia in 1995, to Kosovo in 1999, concluding (after a fashion) with Afghanistan in 2001-02, the United States achieved fair facsimiles of victory.[14] Given the absence of any such facsimile, fair or otherwise, from 1945 to 1991, this was a notable reversal of strategic fortune. Had the U.S. military machine improved dramatically, or had its political masters at last been able to select cooperatively inept foes? Wherever the truth may lie, and I suspect it reposes in a combination of military professional excellence, technological superiority, and enemy incompetence, victory became a habit, indeed was the expectation, over the past decade—at least until now.

Hubris Invites Nemesis.[15] The decade that opened with victory over the USSR, and with a campaign in the Gulf memorialized immodestly and contentiously for the U.S. Army by Major General Robert Scales in a book titled *Certain Victory,* and by Norman Friedman for the U.S. Navy in *Desert Victory,* closed with what appeared to be another brilliant success, this time in Central Asia.[16] For the fourth time in 10 years, American airpower delivered military success, most recently (2001-02) in a style of joint warfare that was as novel as it was appealing to a country still nervous of committing large forces on the ground in distant climes. Both America's friends and foes have noticed a certain military triumphalism about U.S. policy. The George W. Bush administration, in particular, is the beneficiary and the victim of recent military success. It is the beneficiary of a recently acquired (and well-merited) reputation for military effectiveness, as befits the contemporary hegemon. As with Rome in its early imperial centuries, America today is unchallengeable in regular

4

warfare. Also as with Rome, however, a mixture of unusual incompetence, bad luck, and a smart enemy can produce the occasional imperial disaster (happily, Mogadishu was only a minor embarrassment compared with Publius Quintilius Varus's loss of three legions in the Teutoberger Wald in 9 AD). Those whom the Gods would destroy, they first make overweeningly proud. The so-miscalled "war against terrorism"[17] (apart from being a linguistic atrocity) has been launched by an understandably vengeful American hegemon that today is the victim both of its recent military successes and of its own growing conviction that in practice the age-old lore of strategy can be short-circuited by high technology.

Osama bin Laden may or may not prove to be nemesis for American strategic hubris, but he and the elements he represents are likely to show up some contemporary leading American attitudes for what they are, as examples of what historians have called "victory disease."[18] Germany in 1940-41 and Japan in 1942 both fell victim to the illusion of their own invincibility, an illusion fed by the misreading of the causes of their early successes. A new American way of war was demonstrated in Afghanistan, one which married long-range airpower, space systems, special operations forces (SOF), and local allies. But success in Afghanistan may tell us more about the hapless Taleban and its al-Qaeda co-belligerents, than it does about a plausible high road to victory in future conflicts. If, as I beg leave to doubt, the misnamed war against terrorism is World War III, as Lawrence Freedman speculates,[19] the decade of victory from Kuwait City to Kabul is likely to come to a crashing halt. It is perhaps ironic, if not actually unfair, that a hegemonic United States, preeminent in the most advanced ways of regular warfare, should twice be thwarted strategically; first after 1945 by its own nuclear discovery,[20] and now today by exceptionally asymmetrical enemies. The long nuclear stand-off challenged traditional understanding of victory, as goal and as descriptor. The new stand-off between the asymmetrical strategic cultures of hegemonic superpower and transnational terrorism similarly throws into question both the meaning of victory and the sense in its pursuit as high policy, grand strategy, and operational art.

I have chosen not to trouble these opening paragraphs with scholarly quibbles about the definition of terms. Such casualness cannot be indulged any longer, however, because we will be unable to proceed very far down the road to decisive victory unless we are clear enough in our own minds as to just what conditions are and are not, consistent with that destination.

The Big Ideas.

In his book, *The Age of Battles,* Russell F. Weigley argues the case against war as an instrument of decision. Quoting Walter Millis, Weigley writes: "If 'its power of decision' was the 'one virtue' that war had ever had, then war never had any virtue."[21] Referring to the strategic history of 1631 to 1815, "the age of battles," from Breitenfeld to Waterloo, Weigley offers an uncompromising condemnation. "If wars remained incapable of producing decisions at costs proportionate to their objects even then, consequently the whole history of war must be regarded as a history of almost unbroken futility. So it has been." [22] Or has it? I will argue that Weigley is fundamentally wrong. There may well be wars that the belligerents, perhaps all the belligerents, wished they had never entered, but that is another matter entirely. The issue at this juncture in our analysis pertains strictly to the alleged futility of war.

Of course, if war is judged futile if it fails to produce some ideal, enduring, and preferably intended, outcome, then the skeptic has a point. Such an extreme and unrealistic test of war's merit, however, plainly cannot be a test with utility to reasonable people. Historically well-educated persons, certainly those raised in some variant of the "realist" school of statecraft, know that we cannot wage war to end all war, or to establish a permanent universal empire and imperium.[23] Even modest aspirations for a "Thousand-Year Reich" fell 988 years short of the declared ambition. War is a social institution, employed and misemployed by flawed people for a host of reasons, praiseworthy and otherwise. Any rapid foray into the morass of scholarship on the subject of the origins or causes of war or wars impresses with the near unmanageable richness of variety in the subject.[24] War is certainly the most extreme among Man's behaviors, but its history does not suggest that it is beyond the pale of reason, or useful achievement, in high policy. We will argue that Weigley, for all his high reputation as a military historian, was monumentally in error—for then, for today, and for the future—when he took issue with Clausewitz in the following way:

> War in the age of battles was not an effective extension of policy by other means. With partial exceptions encompassing those powers that like Great Britain could sometimes remain on war's periphery and even fight it by proxy, war was not the extension of policy but the bankruptcy of policy.[25]

Famously, Clausewitz wrote that "war is simply a continuation of political intercourse, with the addition of other means."[26] Weigley is right in pointing to the frequency with which the prosecution of war disappoints belligerents, though that is scarcely a dazzling insight. Not infrequently, battlefield achievement is squandered by incompetence in peacemaking. That, however, cannot be a charge leveled at war itself. The nonsense of Weigley's argument is readily demonstrated with reference to the strategic history of the past 100 years. In support of my contention that war is a powerful and effective instrument of decision, albeit not always the decision that we prefer, consider this short list of examples:

- World War I (the numeral was employed, pessimistically, as early as 1920) *decided* that Wilhelmine Germany would not secure European hegemony. Germany did not go to war in pursuit of such a dominant position, but that would have been

7

the consequence had the Central Powers been victorious. The conflict also *decided* definitively the fate of the Austro-Hungarian, Russian, and Ottoman empires.

- World War II *decided* that the Nazi adventure in racial hegemony would come to an abrupt and well-merited conclusion after only 12 years.

- The Korean War, 1950-53, *decided* that forcible unification of the peninsula was not attainable at bearable cost to either side. It would not be correct to claim that 3 years of war—actually 1 year of quite intensive combat followed by 2 years of 'negotiating' and fighting—simply confirmed the *status quo ante*. Prior to June 1950, both North and South, and some among their backers abroad, could aspire not unreasonably to redraw the local geopolitical map along more favored lines.

- The American war in Vietnam, 1965-73, *decided* that South Vietnam would not sustain itself as an independent polity. Although the military decision eventually was lost by America's dependent ally, the protracted U.S. involvement had the effect of *deciding* that communist victory would be delayed by 10 years. That decision for delay, though ultimately unavailing for South Vietnam, may well have played a vitally positive role in the stability and development of South East Asia more broadly. The history of that region subsequent to 1975 suggests that, at least for once in its experience, the United States may have lost the war, but won the peace.

- The Cold War, the virtual World War III, *decided* that the great communist experiment would self-destruct, admittedly with no little assistance from American statecraft. The outcome of this conflict also *decided*,

8

by geopolitical elimination, that the United States would enjoy globally hegemonic status for a while.

- The war over Kosovo in 1999 *decided* whose writ would run in that Yugoslavian province, and in its consequences, it decided also that Slobodan Milosevic and his appalling family would cease to reign and rule in Belgrade.

- The war against the Taleban and al-Qaeda in Afghanistan in 2001 *decided* that that country (speaking loosely) would have a change in central government and probably a return to traditional warlordism, Afghan-style. More to the point, the U.S.-led and enabled military effort decided that Afghanistan is unlikely to provide a safe haven for transnational terrorists for some time to come.

I submit that these seven examples of recent wars demonstrating a significant power of decision are not exceptions that prove a rule to the contrary, affirming war's alleged futility. Naturally, war is apt to be futile, or more likely worse, for the losing side. But the thesis that war either has lost its presumed erstwhile power of decision or, following Weigley, never had such power, is thus easily shown to be absurd. We would not sound the trumpet so loudly on this point, were it not so central to the Big Ideas that must organize this analysis. After all, it is my contention: (a) that wars can be won or lost (admittedly on a sliding scale of completeness, perhaps "decisiveness"); and (b) that wars' outcomes typically have a significant power of decision, if not always the decisions intended, even by the victor. As a corollary to those points, I must insist that war remains not merely useful, but quite literally essential as a tool of statecraft for which there are no close substitutes. Furthermore, rejecting out of hand the proposition that war is futile because it lacks the power of decision, I must insist also that it matters greatly who wins and who loses; in other words, which decisions will a particular war's outcome facilitate and which inhibit.

9

The time is perhaps long overdue for this monograph to deal directly with the key concepts, or Big Ideas, misuse of which fuels confusion and even friction in the policy process.[27] Our North Star is the composite idea(s) of decisive victory. Thus far, we have chosen to treat this very Big Idea in relatively low key, requiring of it only that it recognizes both the likelihood of wars having winners and losers, and the strong probability that the outcomes of wars will, in strategic and political effect, achieve noteworthy decisions. So much should not really be in contention among reasonable people. However, there will always be a rump of idealists who emotionally resist the idea that war is an instrument of policy.

The Big Idea of decisive victory can be disaggregated as above, where it is interpreted in a closely Clausewitzian vein as referring to the ability of success and failure in war to enable issues to be decided (e.g., who runs Kosovo, Europe, or the world!). That approach to the concept should not be unduly controversial. More challenging, perhaps, is a strict focus on the adjectival modifier. What do we think we know, not about the ability of victory to facilitate important (say, geopolitical, or ideological) decisions, but rather about the more or less decisive quality of victory? Braving the risks of damage by some critic wielding Occam's razor, we can argue, following Clausewitz in his belated recognition of real war, that at least three related concepts require explicit recognition. These are not fine academic distinctions, but rather real-world conditions apt to be encountered, indeed enforced, by American superpower. The three concepts are *decisive victory*, which is our organizing Big Idea, *strategic success*, and *strategic advantage*. They comprise a simple three-level view of relative military achievement. By way of clarification, Scales could rightly puff the U.S. Army's achievement in Desert Storm with his tale of *Certain Victory*, but few people 10 years on from that celebration of American military prowess would be completely comfortable with a claim for decisive victory. Unless, of course, one is fairly relaxed about just what it was that was decided. Undoubtedly, a decisive victory was secured in 1991 in terms of the explicit war aims of the Coalition. Victory decided that Kuwaiti oil, let alone Saudi oil, would not enrich Iraq. Also, the war and its consequences decided that the Iraqi path to achievement of deliverable weapons of mass destruction would be extraordinarily long, costly, and painful. Contrary to U.S. hopes and expectations, though, what the war did not decide was a political future for Iraq innocent of Saddam Hussein and led by people committed to a view of regional order that would be judged constructive in Washington.

We can identify several possible meanings to the concept of decisive victory. It might be employed with operational, strategic, or political meaning.

At the operational level, decisive victory should refer to a victory which decides the outcome to a campaign, though not necessarily to the war as a whole. A decisive victory in one theater might be offset by a decisive defeat in another. In contrast, a strategically decisive victory should be one that decides who wins the war militarily. Such a victory or defeat need not be effected by a single climactic clash of arms, but may rather be the outcome of an attritional struggle. Some historians have commented that there were no decisive battles in the two world wars, of necessity both were conducted as long wearing-out processes.[28] That view probably is an exaggeration, though it does point correctly to the great resilience and depth of mobilizable assets of modern societies. It is tempting to identify the German defeats on the Marne in 1914, in the Battle of Britain in 1940, in front of Moscow in 1941, and at Stalingrad in 1942, at least as candidates for "decisive" status. Each of the defeats just cited arguably had some far reaching power of decision over the subsequent course of military events. Politically understood, a decisive victory should be one that enables achievement of a favorable postwar settlement. The quotation from Clausewitz that heads this monograph makes the point exactly. "The political object" should "determine both the military objective to be reached and the amount of effort required." Since soldiers do not make policy, whether or not a military victory is decisive in this political sense is above their pay grade. However, it is the responsibility of the soldier to advise policymakers as to what military power can and cannot accomplish. Also, it is important that war should not be conducted in such a manner as to subvert the prospects for lasting peace.[29]

Victory and defeat register on a sliding scale of possibilities. But a simple axis would miss much of the relevant action. Note Michael Howard's plausible opinion that "a war, fought for whatever reason, that does not aim at a solution which takes into account the fears, the interests and, not least, the honour of the defeated peoples is unlikely to decide anything for very long."[30] Decisive victory probably is sought because we intend to shape the postwar environment for a tolerably good fit with our idea of an international order that provides a lasting condition of peace with security. Though, we must admit, decisive victory also may be sought for the dominant, though not sole, reason of national honor, as in the U.S. case after September 11, 2001.

Although the concept of decisive victory in principle is distinguishable from strategic success or strategic advantage, in practice either of the two more modest achievements can be positively decisive. We may not, indeed generally will not, need to "render the enemy powerless," in order "to impose our will on the enemy."[31] After all, and notwithstanding its declamatory appeal, a decisive victory strictly refers to favorable military achievement which forwards achievement of the war's "political object." Strategic success or strategic advantage, accomplishments that fall notably short of the forcible disarmament of the enemy, may well qualify for the label of decisive victory. Most belligerents seek an end to hostilities well before the point where their power to resist is totally dismantled.[32] The idea of decisive victory, therefore, should not be equated necessarily with the military obliteration of the enemy. All that it requires is a sufficiency of military success to enable achievement of whatever it is that policy identifies as the war's political object.

Military Decision for Political Decision.

Given that most wars are not waged for unlimited goals, whether or not military victory proves politically decisive will be an issue for the (somewhat) defeated party to resolve. North Vietnam and its southern proxies were defeated militarily in 1968 and again in 1972, but in neither case did Hanoi choose to regard the defeat as decisive.[33] In 1940-41, Germany won a succession of military victories that appeared to many people at the time, and not least to the Germans themselves, to be strategically, rather than merely operationally, decisive. North Vietnam in 1968 and 1972, Britain in 1940 (in continental warfare), and the USSR in 1941, all declined to define military failure as political defeat. British and Soviet geography, and U.S. policy guidance for rules of engagement, allowed the losing side to rally, recover, and return to fight again. These historical examples illustrate a structural problem for the strategist.

Strategy is, or should be, a purpose-built bridge linking military power to political goals.[34] If the political aim in war is a total one—the enemy's overthrow—then it has to be matched with a military effort intended to achieve the complete defeat of the foe. We may argue about the respective merits of some apparently contrasting styles in warfare, alternative modes designed to succeed by maneuver, by attrition, or by paralysis. But, we will be in the relatively straightforward realm of military science. We will not be attempting to coerce a reluctant and culturally alien enemy, rather we will be applying such military means as should prove necessary to remove his power of resistance. As I have argued elsewhere, an important reason why strategy is difficult to do well is its very nature as a bridge between military power and policy.[35]

Defense officials have to pretend that they know "how much is enough," so that they can justify the precise numbers proposed in budget requests. Except for the leading luminaries of the McNamara years in the Pentagon, however, American strategic thinkers have rarely been confused over the fact that estimates of "sufficiency" owe more to art than they do to science.[36] Even the carefully calculated drawdown curves of the endless vulnerability analyses that accompanied the competition in strategic arms were exercises in a spurious precision. Those U.S. Cold War strategic calculations were as fundamentally flawed as was Graf von Schlieffen's great final memorandum of December 1905, which neglected logistics, numbers, the French railroads, and Russian recovery from its contemporary low ebb. Modern scholarship has revealed that the so-called "Schlieffen Plan" was in fact nothing more than a speculative think piece, a *Denkschrift*.[37]

It is a most inconvenient fact that "[W]ar is nothing but a duel on a larger scale." Clausewitz explains that:

> If you want to overcome your enemy you must match your effort against his power of resistance, which can be expressed as the product of two inseparable factors, *viz. The total means at his disposal and the strength of his will.* The extent of the means at his disposal is a matter—though not exclusively—of figures, and should be measurable. But the strength of his will is much less easy to determine and can only be gauged approximately by the strength of the motive animating it.[38]

The meaning, perhaps meanings, ascribed to decisive victory assume huge significance in the light of Clausewitz's words. By way of an elementary two dimensional cut at the issue: the quest for decisive victory may focus either on the apparent completeness of the military success—meaning that a victory is militarily decisive—or on the quality and quantity of political decision that that military victory enables. Although the former must underpin the latter, a focus on victory as contrasted with the political fruits of victory desired by policy translates all too readily into the situation where war obeys the dictates of its own nature. "That while the purpose of war is to serve a political end, the nature of war is to serve itself."[39] Military victory becomes an end in itself, and policy is shaped to assist the war effort, rather than vice versa.

Because strategy is a highly imprecise art, albeit one subject to some material discipline (e.g., with reference to logistics), calculation of what is required to deliver victory is never going to be better than guesswork. In principle, at least, a proximate goal of military overthrow does usefully simplify matters, in that the overriding problems should be fairly strictly military in character. If, however, policy specifies restricted political goals, which logically should require the application only of limited military power, the full challenge to strategy is easily comprehended. Defined as the use that is made of force and the threat of force for the ends of policy, strategy is not always a bridge in good repair. Strategy is neither the use of force nor the ends of policy, but somehow, mysteriously, it is the employment of the former to satisfy the latter. The more modest the policy goals, and hence the more measured the military action, presumably the greater the policy discretion an enemy enjoys.

For a contrary, counterfactual example, in 1964-65 the United States might have decided that its modest objective, to preserve a noncommunist South Vietnam, could be secured only if North Vietnam was rendered physically incapable of waging, or supporting, war in the South. Rather than engage in a battle of wills, the United States would have sought to deny Hanoi the ability to fight in the South, regardless of the strength of its political will. Contemporary American limited war theory, drafted by civilian theorists and not by soldiers, was not friendly to the proposition that sledge hammers made good nut crackers.[40] The consequence was a 10-year conflict wherein the United States indulged in what Thomas C. Schelling called at the time "the diplomacy of violence."[41] The war could be lost, but not won, in South Vietnam alone. For a range of reasons, persuasive and otherwise, the United States elected to fight a limited war in a distinctly limited way.[42] The Gods of War are not thus to be mocked. The outcome was determined by the test of political wills that the United States had promoted to pole position by its determination to wage only a limited war in the South and over the North.

To achieve a decisive military victory that would have taken North Vietnam out of the war (for a long while to come, at least), could only have been a most challenging and perilous, though feasible, undertaking. But the quest for decisive victory along the strategic road actually taken stood very little chance of succeeding. The reason, of course, was that too much policy discretion was allowed to an enemy whose political motivation was of the highest order, and whose resources for war were not sufficiently damaged. The American theory and practice of limited conventional war proved unduly eloquent in appreciation of the merit in limitations on the use of force, and inadequately appreciative of what Clausewitz termed the "grammar" of war.[43] Rephrased, there are times when the prudent path to relatively modest policy goals should be taken by what appear to be disproportionately muscular military efforts. A defense community whose best and brightest theorists were civilian academics was understandably slow in grasping that point. The "principles of war," though much maligned by defense intellectuals in the 1950s and 1960s,[44] were neglected in the U.S. conduct of war in Vietnam, with most unhappy consequences.

There is not much about war that is literally, as opposed to merely rhetorically, calculable. Logistical problems are, indeed have to be, calculable, though there was a Napoleonic and later German approach to the challenge of supply and movement which transcended boldness and ventured far into irresponsibility.[45] Even the sums of the logisticians, however, are subject to practical refutation by the action of "friction" of many kinds—for example, bad weather, mechanical breakdown, unexpectedly unfriendly terrain, including insect life and disease[46]—and particularly to harassing efforts by the enemy. It is surprising how many otherwise impressive examples of military planning betray a pervasive failure to recognize that war is, alas, a duel.

The strategist must cope with an uncertain exchange rate between military effort and political effect. If the overthrow of the enemy is not the policy goal, the strength and durability under pressure of his political will must be a crucial determinant of whether or not a decisive victory is achievable at tolerable cost. We may be denied practicable attainment of decisive victory if the enemy chooses not to be coerced into acquiescence by the amount and kinds of military pressure that we allow ourselves to apply.[47] This was the U.S. problem in Vietnam. The logic of decisive victory in limited war is generically identical to the logic of success in deterrence. In both cases, the enemy has to choose to cooperate, albeit under duress, if we are to claim some variant of decisive success. He can choose to fight on, calculating that the political decision we seek will be judged by us not to be worth the human, economic, and political costs of protracted, and possibly more intense, combat.

By way of a rather extreme historical illustration of the argument, in 1941 Imperial Japan chose to wage a necessarily limited war against the United States. The Japanese adventure rested on the calculation, hopeful guess perhaps, that its immediate military victories would translate into a political decision by a Washington focused on Germany in Europe to acquiesce in Japan's conquests. This hideous miscalculation had its roots in a misreading of American culture, and an underestimation of American mobilization potential. To compound their sins against the lore of strategy, the Japanese succumbed prematurely to a bad case of "victory fever."[48] The lore of strategy includes injunctions about relating means to ends and the necessity to exercise choice in resource allocation between competing operational possibilities. Imperial Japan was not fundamentally misinformed about U.S. military potential, though the scale and rate of realization of that potential were a surprise to the whole world. Rather, its cardinal error was cultural and political. Tokyo failed to appreciate that the attack on the U.S. Pacific Fleet at Pearl Harbor would be a full frontal assault upon American honor. That was the kind of action that could not readily be tidied up politically by means of some compromise agreement, let alone by an injured America acquiescing in Japanese aggression. This admittedly extreme example nonetheless demonstrates with great clarity how difficult it can be to cash tactical and operational military success in the coin of lasting political advantage. Al-Qaeda and its friends and allies inadvertently may have made the same miscalculation in 2001 as did Japan in 1941. In both cases, the political consequences of military action probably were not those anticipated by the aggressor.

Before we turn to consider how decisive victory is more, and less, likely to be achieved, three broad propositions need stating.

First, decisive victory, and indecisive victory even more so, is hard to translate into desired political effect. Clausewitz rightly insists that "at the highest level the art of war turns into policy—but a policy conducted by fighting battles rather than by sending diplomatic notes."[49] He does not dwell, however, on the difficulties that beset the strategist on the bridge between military power and policy. The concept of strategic effect usefully conflates the consequences of the threat and use of force of all kinds, so that we have a common currency for the value of all forms of military power.[50] What we do not have, to repeat the point, is an agreed exchange rate between apparent military success and political reward. "War" comes in many shapes and forms, has many different contexts, and is subject to diverse cultural influences. As the writings of Victor Davis Hanson explain, culturally asymmetrical belligerents are apt to disagree on the definition, feasibility, and consequences of so-called decisive victory.[51] British historian Jeremy Black registers the same argument when he claims that "war and success in war are cultural constructs."[52]

Second, decisive victory is probably best viewed as a range of possibilities, rather than as a stark alternative to the failure to achieve such a success. The enemy can be understood to have continuing powers of resistance on a sliding scale. Decisive victories come in many guises and sometimes mislead the winner. Cannae was the tactically decisive victory straight from the textbook, but its operational, strategic, and political consequences were trivial.[53] Roman civic militarism produced fresh legions. Hannibal could win battles; indeed, for a long period, he and his veteran mercenaries and his barbarian allies tactically were invincible, but he lacked a convincing theory of victory in war as a whole. Moving very fast forward, Jutland in May 1916 was a material, though not tactical or operational, victory for Germany's High Seas Fleet. It was a strategically decisive victory for the Royal Navy, however, because its very occurrence and its course demonstrated to the German Government that its fleet could not challenge Britain in the North Sea for the right to use the seas. Jutland was widely interpreted in Britain at the time as a significant defeat. In May-June 1940, the Wehrmacht won what many contemporary commentators regarded as a decisive victory over France and Britain. The victory decided that France, if not all of its empire, was definitively *hors de combat*. The most important decisive effect of the victory, however, was its influence on German self-evaluation in general, and the Fuhrer's self-confidence as warlord in particular. What the victory decided was that Germany would judge itself militarily unbeatable in continental warfare. The planning for Operation BARBAROSSA, and then the (mis)conduct of that campaign from June to December 1941, showed the effect of the "decisive" victory of May-June 1940.[54]

Third, even if we affirm that decisive victory is our doctrine and military intention, in practice, a number of degrees of decisiveness are likely to prove acceptable. That may not be the case if we are waging a total war keyed to the goal of enforced régime change, though even then a change in regime leadership effected by internal convulsion might tempt us to moderate our strategic goals. American analysts and officials must recognize that one size does not fit all when it comes to conceptualizing about "war," or to estimating the likely military effectiveness of particular capabilities. Again to quote Jeremy Black, war has "multiple contexts."[55] A simple style in warfare which worked well against the Taleban, though less well against al-Qaeda in the context of Afghan politics, is not necessarily reliably applicable in other contexts. War against Saddam Hussein's Iraq, against the Taleban in Afghanistan, and now against terrorism, world-wide, are all notably distinctive enterprises. If regime change in Baghdad and Kabul counts as decisive victory—to ignore the more troubling political difficulties that must follow such successes—what would constitute decisive victory over, say, al-Qaeda, let alone "terrorism" in general? Decisive victory is possible against terrorists, but it is not the kind of victory that can be practiced in the California desert. Doctrine and metrics of success have to be tailored to the character of warfare at issue.

Achieving Decisive Victory.

We reject as arrant nonsense the view expressed by the British socialist and pacifist, George Lansbury, when on September 3, 1939, he claimed that "in the end force has not settled, and cannot and will not settle anything."[56] It is not entirely true to argue, for example, that a bad idea can only be defeated by a better idea. There are times, as from 1939 to 1945, when a particularly bad idea—Hitler's vision of a racially pure Thousand Year Reich—needs to be shot. Nazi ideology could not be tamed by any peaceful process of political or cultural engagement.[57] If occasionally force must be used, it is important to win and, to go back a step, it is necessary to know how to win. War may be the realm of chance, as Clausewitz advises,[58] but victory or defeat are not recorded as random outcomes. There is an approach to war that maximizes the prospect of the achievement of decisive victory (whatever outcome one decides is sufficiently decisive and adequately victorious). That approach is best expressed in just five propositions, which can be phrased both negatively as caveats, or positively as advice for action.

1. ***Better armies tend to win***. Contrary to Clausewitz's metaphor, war is not like a game of cards.[59] One's military "hand" is not dealt at random. Friction and surprise by enemy moves certainly can render campaign plans obsolete before the computer's printer has cooled, but armies who understand the nature of war expect to have to adapt in realtime to circumstances that could not have been forecast with precision long in advance. There are objectively superior and inferior armies. Armies that recruit with high standards, train hard and realistically, keep tight discipline, equip intelligently, enjoy some measure of luck, and study their variety of opponents each on its own terms, will tend to win. Because surprise is always possible, even probable, an important quality in a better army is its ability to find a way to win, its capability to adjust to unexpected events when plans are rendered obsolete by the independent will of the foe. As General Dwight D. Eisenhower once observed, the principal value of military planning is not to produce ahead of time the perfect plan, but rather to train planners who can adjust and adapt to changing circumstances as they emerge.

The achievement of decisive victory at bearable cost can rarely be guaranteed, but we can raise and maintain an army that is objectively superior in relevant quality and quantity. A good army is not one developed for its specialized excellence in a particular scenario, unless, that is, a country's defense planners are sufficiently fortunate as to have a truly dominant threat in their present and confidently anticipated future. Because war is not solitaire, even an excellent army may fail to deliver victory. Policy simply may ask too much of its military instrument, or it may hamstring military operations with damaging political constraints. The German Army in both world wars set the contemporary standard for tactical and operational

21

excellence. But in war after war, German policy asked its soldiers to accomplish the impossible. To try to win against a coalition greatly superior in resources, in circumstances where dazzling operational maneuver is infeasible, means condemnation to a lengthy struggle. When war is protracted, military skills tend to equalize among belligerents, and brute numbers count for more and more as the smaller side is less and less able to absorb a high rate of casualties. In both world wars, the Germans trained their enemies. By the Summer and Fall of 1918, the British Army was tactically at least as competent as the by then much weakened Germans, especially with respect to the scientific use of artillery;[60] while by 1944-45 the Soviet Army had taken operational art to a level not attained even by the Wehrmacht at its peak.[61]

To summarize this discussion, we are likely to achieve decisive victories if our army meets universally valid standards of military excellence (e.g., if discipline is tight, training is tough, morale is high, equipment is reliable and modern, logistics are well-prepared, and so forth). However, decisive victory may well elude us, notwithstanding our apparent military excellence, if the army is too small, if it is assigned missions for which it is ill-fitted, or if politicians insist upon shaping military operations according to extra-military criteria (e.g., do not provoke Chinese intervention in Vietnam) in defiance of the "grammar" of war. It might be needless to add that even a first-rate military instrument will fail to bring home the bacon if it is mishandled by poor generalship, either at the level of operations or tactically in battle. The French army at Ligny–Quatre Bras–Waterloo in June 1815 was by no means Napoleon's finest. It was, however, by quite a margin the best army then in the field—superior to Blucher's Prussians and to Wellington's mixed cohorts of British, Dutch, Belgian, and German soldiers. Deficiencies in the French performance of command, operationally and tactically, delivered Wellington and Blucher a genuinely decisive military victory.[62] To bring the story more up-to-date, it could be argued that poor Anglo-American generalship in the Summer of 1944 allowed too much of the beaten German Army to escape both from Normandy and then from France, to rally for the defense of the Reich. Moving on 6 years, General MacArthur's conduct of the invasion of North Korea affronted most of the principles of war, with dire consequences for troops of the United Nations (U.N.) Command. With reference to the mid- and late 1960s, although scapegoats abounded for the disappointing course of the war in Vietnam, it is difficult to resist the judgment that a fine American army was poorly directed in the field.

2. *No magic formula for victory.* War is so serious, complex, and uncertain an undertaking that its practitioners and interpreters are always on the alert for some "key" to victory, some philosopher's stone for military art. Henri Jomini's popularity with 19th-century soldiers is entirely understandable. Instead of the somewhat opaque Clausewitzian strictures about friction and chance, Jomini offered a delightful certainty. "Correct theories, founded upon right principles, sustained by actual events of wars, and added to accurate military history, will form a true school of instruction for generals."[63] At the heart of Jomini's system, at least of his reading of Napoleonic practice, was what he called the "one great principle underlying all the operations of war—a principle which must be followed in all good combinations."[64] The principle was the injunction, *inter alia*, to throw superior force at inferior force (at the "decisive point" and at the decisive time), so that the enemy, even if numerically superior overall, can be defeated in detail, and to threaten his lines of communication. A problem was that Napoleon Bonaparte, on a good day at least, could be inventive. Sometimes he would attempt his signature *manoeuvre sur les derrières,* and sometimes he would not. The truth is that Napoleon did not have a doctrine, a formula, for victory.

The quest for the key to certain victory can lead strategists astray. Alfred von Schlieffen's approach was founded upon meticulous timetabling and confident

23

projections even of the operational end-game.[65] That particular German school of General Staff thinking was not interested in political context, logistical problems, or the need to improvise and adapt should the enemy not behave as expected. In his brilliant essay on Jomini, John Shy noted that modern American strategic analysis had located the certainty it craved.[66] In the spirit of Jomini's "one great principle," American arms controllers, for example, had found universal strategic truth in a formula for stability. Every strategic weapon system could be analyzed according to whether or not it contributed to, or detracted from, stability. Though bereft of political, or indeed common, sense, this stability theory was revealed truth to many in the 1970s and 1980s.

Today, much of the enthusiasm for the information-led revolution in military affairs (RMA), or military transformation (as the newly preferred term of art), stems from that same yearning for military certainty. The Gulf War model of decisive action appeared to demonstrate how total victory could be achieved reliably in the future. Events in the succeeding decade have done little to shake faith in the ideology of victory through technology. Somalia in 1993-94 might have prompted more soul searching than seems to have occurred, but Bosnia in 1995, Kosovo in 1999, and Afghanistan in 2001-02, have all been interpreted as evidence confirming the soundness of the new American RMA'd way of war. Strategic history tries to tell us that wars come in a wide variety of forms and are waged in all manner of terrain. Because, to repeat, all wars are duels, eventually technological formulae (indeed, any formula) for decisive victory will fail. The failure will be the result of tactical ineffectiveness in specific circumstances (e.g., in an urban setting), or operational and strategic negation by an enemy who behaves as Edward Luttwak predicts in his masterwork on strategy.[67] The paradoxical logic of conflict states that what works today will not work tomorrow, because it worked today. In short, formulaic military behavior can be deadly when the foe is intelligent and even just moderately capable.

3. ***Technology is not a panacea***. The attractive proposition that the United States currently enjoys an unassailable military technological lead which has sharply reduced the value of allies, and which can deliver decisive victory more or less to order, is fragile or wrong on all counts.[68] Technology is only one of strategy's dimensions, and it is by no means the most important. The Fulleresque belief that relative technological prowess is the prime determinant of strategic success has a substantial problem with the historical record in all periods.[69] It is difficult to find clear examples of decisive victories in war achieved because of a superiority in weaponry. We must hasten to add the caveats that always are provided: either the belligerents were technologically in touch with each other (i.e., not assegais against maxim guns); or, even if they were truly far apart in mastery of war's machines, the materially challenged party sought and found effective asymmetrical offsets.

When a capability appears almost too good to be true, especially when it pertains to an activity as complex, uncertain, and risky as war, the odds are that, indeed, it is too good to be true. If technology gives us an edge, then by all means let us welcome and exploit it. But the American military record from 1991 to the present should not be misread as convincing evidence of the emergence of a new way to the reliable achievement of decisive victory. Bombardment, no matter how precise, is not synonymous with war as a whole. The notion that the United States has stumbled upon a technological formula for decisive victory with its still largely unreconstructed military establishment, should be met with a healthy skepticism. The "Afghan model," wherein special operations forces team with (generally) long-range airpower and unmanned aerial vehicles (UAVs) for the precise delivery of JDAMS, all in aid of the taking of territory by local allies, may be hard to replay elsewhere.

History provides by far the largest strike against the belief that a transformed U.S. military, one that is the global leader by a country mile in providing information-led and well-networked RMA'd forces, has unlocked the secret of decisive victory. Technology is only one among the many dimensions of strategy and war. American optimists should be sobered by the datum that weapons do not win wars, not excluding superior weapons. Furthermore, even when new technology is weaponized in appropriate quantity, employed by intelligently tailored organizations, and is directed by suitable doctrine, it is still no guarantor of decisive victory. The reasons lie in the complexity of war, the options probably open to the enemy, and that hardy perennial, friction. There can always be a first time for an important development, but it is difficult to identify a war, let alone a succession of wars, in modern history wherein exploitation of a technological lead plainly was chiefly responsible for victory. Norman Schwarzkopf was characteristically emphatic in his claim that the coalition would have won the Gulf War even had the two sides swapped equipment. Germany did not lose two world wars because of technological lags. There is a sense in which the USSR lost the Cold War because of its inability to compete technologically,[70] but the critical Soviet competitive disadvantages lay in the realms of tired ideology and unduly comfortable party-industrial bureaucrats.

What matters most is how weapons are used, and by whom. The United States is riding for a most painful fall if it proceeds into this new century confident that its military hegemony is secured for decades to come by its current military technological lead. The U.S. Army should recall the limited, albeit still real, utility of its bright and shiny new air mobility concept in Vietnam in the 1960s,[71] while the Soviet Army scarcely fared much better in Afghanistan in the 1980s.[72] The tools of war are important, but typically they are not the drivers to victory. Alfred Thayer Mahan provided a wise comment for the ages when he wrote:

> Historically, good men with poor ships are better than poor men with good ships; over and over again the French Revolution taught this lesson, which our own age, with its rage for the last new thing in material improvement, has largely dropped out of memory.[73]

Technophiles should ponder also the culturalist thesis advanced by Victor Davis Hanson, though they can take some comfort from his argument.

> It is one argument of this book that the Western way of war is grounded not merely in technological supremacy but in an entire array of political, social and cultural institutions that are responsible for military advantages well beyond the possession of sophisticated weapons.[74]

A defense community that rests its faith for future success in a lasting technological lead will be apt to be vulnerable on several counts. Specifically, technological prowess will tend to equalize among polities over time, especially when, as today, much of the frontier technology is civilian in origin and can be acquired off the shelf;[75] asymmetrical doctrines and practices of war may reduce the value of high technology weaponry quite sharply; the political and geographical contexts of conflicts may demand manpower intensive operations rather than precise firepower; a technological hubris could encourage an army to lose its adaptability to different conditions; and, as unsurprisingly has happened in Afghanistan, bombardment can become an end in itself with the conduct of war reduced to the application of firepower.

4. *The complexity of strategy and war is the mother of invention.* Strategy and war have to be approached holistically, all of their dimensions, or elements, are always in play, though not always of equal importance. Nominally, indeed plainly measurably, weaker armies than the American can search for areas of strength to offset their near certain deficiencies in technology.[76] Americans should be well-schooled by their own national history to be alert to the power of smart substitution among war's elements. How

and why did the colonists defeat the might of the British Empire? Why did Confederate resistance last as long as it did and come close to validating by battle the assertions of seccession and independence?

There are problems with the concept of asymmetry in strategic affairs; essentially it is "an empty box" bereft of identifiable meaning.[77] But the concept, for all its opacity and even triviality, does usefully alert people to the potential strategic rewards that can accrue to those who dare to be different. For the time being, the armed forces of the United States, rather like the Roman legions in their heyday, have taken regular symmetrical ways in war out of the active plans of potential enemies. Only seriously psychologically disturbed, martyr-bound leaders are going to tempt American military power with the inviting prospect of "certain victory." Because strategic effectiveness is the product of behavior across all of strategy's dimensions, America's enemies will strive to find and exploit areas of relative strength for the levelling, or better, of the playing field. In Southeast Asia, for example, consider the appalling handicap under which MACV labored, given the sanctuary status of North Vietnam itself, of Laos, and of Cambodia. In the current war against terrorism, if that is what it is, much of America's striking power is going to be hobbled and nobbled by strategy's political dimension. Many states that are not at all friendly to terrorists, especially those who aim at them, are even less friendly to the American practice of hegemonic guardianship of international order.[78]

In their pursuit of decisive victory, the U.S. armed forces should expect to be opposed not only by inept bad guys picked by central casting to play the role of hapless victims of American military excellence. In addition to the rag, tag, and bobtail of fairly regular, and some irregular, forces who presented themselves for defeat and who played a vitally cooperative role in what now is known as "the Afghan model" of future warfare, the United States is likely to have to confront a genuinely smart enemy who understands the full range of grand strategy.[79]

The complexity of strategy, the fact that strategic effectiveness is the conflated consequence of behavior and attributes on many dimensions, can work to America's advantage as well as disadvantage. Asymmetrical conflict is a game that two can play.

All episodes of conflict are struggles between belligerents who seek to substitute strength for weakness in those dimensions where they are at a disadvantage. The limited war literature of the 1950s and 1960s should have been more eloquent than it generally was on the subject of the competitive setting of the limits to military action. How a war is fought, where it is allowed to be fought, with what weapons, and so forth must go a long way to determine the prospects for decisive victory. Some fraction of the combat may be intended to test the emerging limits upon action in quest of more favorable terms of engagement. The U.S. Army needs to be alert to the threat to the prospect of victory that lurks in the potential ability of an enemy to exploit relative strengths on some of strategy's dimensions in order to offset its areas of technological weakness.[80]

5. *Know your enemies.* Respect for the enemy and his way in warfare has not been strongly characteristic of the American military experience. For example, Robert M. Utley's studies of the U.S. Army in the Indian Wars show a military establishment that made few concessions to the practical needs of the conduct of war against irregular foes.[81] In the 20th century, the U.S. Army entered both world wars overconfident in its ability to teach Germans and Japanese the errors of their ways. More recently, initially at least, the enemy in Korea was not highly rated, while in Vietnam the possibility that the North Vietnamese Army and its southern proxies might prove a worthy foe was not taken as seriously as it should have been.[82] Somalia in 1993-94 is almost too obvious and painful an example to cite. Probably the only historical example of the U.S. Army

showing an undue measure of respect for its enemy was in the Eastern theater during the Civil War.

Really good armies are flexible and adaptable to a wide variety of combat conditions. The British Army before World War I was notably short on general doctrine beyond that which could be gleaned from the Field Service Regulations because, as a force with literally global duties, it had to be able to move and fight in all kinds of terrain against vastly different, generally irregular, enemies.[83] The Romans and the Byzantines faced the same problem.[84] The British Army had to be competitive in mountain warfare with tribesmen on India's North-West frontier, while also capable of waging a mobile campaign (largely as mounted infantry) against Boer commandos on the high veldt of Southern Africa.[85] For their part, the Roman legions of the first and second centuries AD proved adept at waging guerrilla warfare, a form of combat socially, logistically, and culturally impracticable for their German enemies.[86]

Sun-tzu advises as follows:

> Thus it is said that one who knows the enemy and knows himself will not be endangered in a hundred engagements. One who does not know the enemy but knows himself will sometimes be victorious, sometimes meet with defeat. One who knows neither the enemy nor himself will invariably be defeated in every engagement.[87]

Just as tactics are easier to perform satisfactorily than is strategy, so the material instruments of war—though, of course, essential—have a way of deflecting attention from the vital human element.[88] Consider the challenge to a policy of deterrence, for a leading example. Frequent reference may be found in official, popular, and even scholarly literature to "the deterrent." Deterrence, which by definition is a relational variable, is equated with the military machines procured for its intended enforcement. But it so happens that decisive victory for deterrence can be achieved only with the admittedly coerced cooperation of the targeted deterree. The path to decisive victory through

30

successful deterrence is likely to lead less through bulking-up our arsenal and rather more through detailed understanding of the intended deterree so that menaces are precisely targeted at values vital to the enemy.

Deterrence will always be an uncertain and unreliable behavior, which can fail for reasons quite beyond the control of rational defense planners.[89] Nonetheless, taking the enemy seriously as a unique political and strategic cultural entity must enhance the prospects of our achieving decisive success. There is no small danger that a succession of easy victories, such as the United States has achieved over the past decade—with the exception of Somalia—will encourage a misleading "technological triumphalism." Military establishments, being sensibly conservative and prudent when offered novelty ("transformation" and the like), can hardly help but seek and apply the lessons learned in recent conflicts. The somewhat autistic tendency understandable in the defense thinking of a superpower is pregnant with peril for the future. The issue can be simplified as the complex question, "did Iraq/Serbia/the Taleban lose the war, or did we win it with our new model of warfare?" It is, I believe, a fact that the United States could not have lost the Gulf War, the war over Kosovo, or the war in Afghanistan. The winning was not always elegant, and the consequences of decisive success often left much to be desired politically, but the prospects for victory were indeed as certain as they could be for this realm of chance.

Any formula for military success invites potential enemies to emulate, to evade, and to offset. Future foes more competent than those encountered of recent years may not perform the role of largely passive victims for the American way in war on the "Afghan model." Also, churlish though it can seem to mention it, the victories recorded since 1991 were achieved despite serious errors of omission and commission which might have proved costly against more worthy opposition. The Gulf War was poorly conducted operationally, with far too much of the regime's Republican Guard being permitted to escape. The air campaign against

Serbia in 1999 over Kosovo was a mixture of strategic irrelevance and tactical failure. The success in Afghanistan in 2001-02 should not be allowed to obscure the fact that the joint and combined military operations have fallen woefully short of reasonable expectations.[90] Aside from the elusiveness of Osama bin Laden, U.S. and allied forces permitted far too many al-Qaeda fighters with heavy equipment to escape from Kandahar. More damning still, the protracted investment and assault upon the Tora Bora and Shah-i-Kot cave complexes appears to have been conducted with little regard to blocking escape routes over the Pakistani frontier. Indeed, the Tora Bora case revealed so great a tactical, perhaps operational, incompetence as to raise the suspicion that the world of high policy did not want a high body-count, dead or as prisoners of war.

My point is not the trivial and rather ungenerous one that mistakes are made in war. Rather, the purpose of the discussion is to remind Americans that for a decade they have been flexing military muscles in exceptionally permissive strategic contexts. Because outcomes reasonably describable as decisively successful were achieved in 1991, 1995, 1999, and 2001-02, courtesy of an airpower-led "transforming" U.S. military, it does not follow that future conflicts must follow the same pattern.

Conclusions.

As a military objective, decisive victory is not controversial. Whether or not the decision sought needs to be conclusive, if not necessarily quite of a Carthaginian character (*Carthago delenda est*), is a matter initially for policy to decide and then for political-military dialogue as events unfold. The quest for decisive success in the 21st century will more and more carry the risk of yielding only a painful Pyrrhic victory, as some of America's enemies prudently equip themselves with weapons of mass destruction. Desperate dictators, recognizing that they stand helplessly on the brink of personal and régime oblivion, may prove to be beyond deterrence or compellence, should the United States give them the choice. The common sense strategic logic of the U.S. commitment to homeland missile defense, as well as to mobile theater missile defense, is too self-evident to require further comment here.

This lengthy exploration of the meaning and achievement of decisive victory yields four claims that merit elevation as concluding thoughts. First, decisive victory is both possible and important, though it is never guaranteed, not even by military-technological excellence. The assertion that war never solves anything, that it is inherently indecisive, is simply wrong. All of history reveals the decision power of the threat or use of force. In a moral sense it may be preferable to talk rather than fight, but the West is unduly inclined to talk when it should be fighting. Bosnia, Kosovo, and al-Qaeda were all instances of enemies who should have been addressed militarily long before they actually were. America's European allies are increasingly nervous of what they discern as an assertive, unilateralist, military triumphalist United States, disinclined either to pursue serious dialogue with potential "rogues" or to live with strategic irritants. Always provided the United States does not truly succumb to its own high-tech variant of that historically familiar malady, "victory disease," it is to be hoped that the anxieties of debellicized allies will not disarm the superpower guardian of the international order.

Second, one size cannot fit all in the deterrence or conduct of war. If the United States were to find in the decades ahead that once again it faced a clearly dominant threat from a great power,[91] probably China or, less plausibly, China and Russia, it might well find itself needing to improvise in real-time. From the Gulf to Afghanistan, via the Balkans, U.S. military power was granted the initiative and generally time to correct for early errors. Most styles in war lack universal applicability. Blitzkrieg worked well enough in restricted terrain against poor French and British armies that compounded their problems in quantity with the commission of disastrous

quality (CG)

operational moves.[92] It worked much less well in Russian terrain against an enemy who declined to acknowledge decisive defeat.[93] If the American way of war becomes formulaic, albeit technologically impressive, it invites smart enemies to attempt to wage the kind of conflict wherein U.S. strengths would be at a heavy discount. Any belief that U.S. military power, somewhat transformed by the exploitation of information systems of all kinds, can plan to fight almost without regard to enemy preferences and abilities, should be hastily buried. Following the Japanese experience (the 1904 and 1941 "model"), for example, it is not likely that China would prove to be a passive foe, content or obliged to fight only on American terms.[94]

Third, decisive victory, though a meaningful concept, is not a clear-cut alternative to defeat, or even to indecisive victory. Both decision and victory register on scales that allow for more and for less. If the ideal type of military encounter which should yield a decisive outcome was the brief but bloody clash of arms between the citizen hoplites of the Greek city states,[95] then the war upon which the United States today says it is embarked is at the opposite end of the spectrum of potential for decision. In words attributed to Mao Tse-tung: "There is in guerrilla warfare no such thing as a decisive battle."[96] Decisive victory needs to be supplemented in American public discourse with the less imperial notions of strategic advantage and strategic success. It is distinctly American to believe that wars should be unmistakably militarily winnable and to be intolerant of apparently indecisive operations.[97] Much as the U.S. defense community had to come to terms with the unique constraints imposed by the emergence in the 1950s of a strategic context of mutual nuclear deterrence, so today it needs to adjust to the frustrating realities of war against transnational terrorist organizations. America's NATO allies, as well as Russia, China, and a host of other polities, have more or less extensive experience of war against, and living with, terrorists. For the United States, notwithstanding the occasional outrage committed by the manic Left and Right—or 30-odd years ago by African-American extremists—the idea of living permanently, if uneasily, with the insecurity of terrorist menace is novel. America's information-led RMA certainly has some utility in the war on terror, particularly for distant surveillance and targeting, but it is not going to deliver anything grander than some strategic success.

Fourth, and finally, the fact of U.S. interest in the concept of decisive victory is in itself politically and culturally revealing. It is difficult to imagine this topic arousing any interest whatsoever in any NATO member other than the United States. The general irrelevance of military power in NATO-European and EU policy calculation, and the comfortable assumption of a coalition context for all military issues, renders the concept of decisive victory a throwback to less happy times for Europeans. It is no exaggeration to say that despite the character of NATO, which is still, just about, a collective defense organization, America's European friends and allies inhabit a universe that poses no serious military questions. It is true that Kosovo in 1999 was a NATO undertaking, but that episode, and indeed the whole sorry ex-Yugoslavian story of the 1990s, showed how far NATO-Europe has travelled down the road leading to military impotence.

There is a time and sometimes a place for insistence upon decisive victory. Europeans, snakebitten by two world wars "at home," are less than intrigued by means and methods to achieve such military success. When Americans encounter honest but culturally alien European disinterest in the capability to achieve decisive victory, they are naturally inclined to suspect allied motives, while breathing a sigh of relief that their preferred way in war really does not require the complication of non-American assistance (local allies are another matter). A problem for the quality of U.S. policy and strategy is that as NATO allies merit less and less military respect in Washington, so their views on global security more and more are discounted. The United States increasingly finds itself strictly in a league of its own, wherein it listens to little but the echo of its own domestic debate about the use of force. Dialogue among unequals is always difficult, but in this case it is urgently needed as the United States embarks upon the first war of the 21st century, if not World War III.

ENDNOTES

1. Raymond Aron, "The Evolution of Modern Strategic Thought," in Alastair Buchan, ed., *Problems of Modern Strategy*, London: ISS, 1970, p. 25.

2. "The Elusive Character of Victory," *The Economist,* November 24, 2001, pp. 11-12; Conrad Black, "What Victory Means," *The National Interest,* No. 66, Winter 2001/02, pp. 155-64.

3. Thomas C. Schelling, *Arms and Influence*, New Haven, CT: Yale University Press, 1966, p. 31.

4. See Azar Gat, *The Origins of Military Thought: From the Enlightenment to Clausewitz*, Oxford: Clarendon Press, 1989, ch. 7, esp. p. 199.

5. Carl von Clausewitz, *On War,* Michael Howard and Peter Paret, eds. and trans., Princeton, NJ: Princeton University Press, 1976, p. 75, emphasis original.

6. Michael Quinlan, *Thinking about Nuclear Weapons*, London: Royal United Services Institute for Defence Studies, 1997, p. 19.

7. Colin S. Gray and Keith B. Payne, "Victory Is Possible," *Foreign Policy,* No. 39, Summer 1980, pp. 14-27. The title, picked by the editor of the journal, would have been improved had the words "but improbable," been added.

8. Colin S. Gray, "Nuclear Strategy: The Case for a Theory of Victory," *International Security,* Vol. 4, No. 9., Summer 1979, pp. 54-87.

9. Edward N. Luttwak, *On the Meaning of Victory: Essays on Strategy*, New York: Simon and Schuster, 1986, p. 289.

10. The commitment to "prevail" in a nuclear war was written in the new *Defense Guidance, 1984-1988,* document which was inevitably

leaked to *The Washington Post*. For a relevant quotation, see Lawrence Freedman, *The Evolution of Nuclear Strategy*, 2nd ed., New York: St. Martin's Press, 1989, p. 406.

11. Casper W. Weinberger, *Annual Report to the Congress, Fiscal Year 1986*, Washington, DC: U.S. Government Printing Office, February 4, 1985, p. 45.

12. Casper W. Weinberger in *The New York Times*, August 9, 1982.

13. For example, Stephen Kotkin, *Armageddon Averted: The Soviet Collapse, 1970-2000*, Oxford: Oxford University Press, 2001. A different opinion animates Peter Schweizer, *Victory: The Reagan Administration's Secret Strategy That Hastened the Collapse of the Soviet Union,* New York: Atlantic Monthly Press, 1994; and William E. Odom, *The Collapse of the Soviet Military,* New Haven, CT: Yale University Press, 1998. Odom notes that "a program of U.S. military modernization based on new technologies confronted the Soviet military with another challenge it could not hope to meet." P. 87.

14. See Mark Bowden, *Black Hawk Down*, London: Bantam Press, 1999, on Somalia; Robert C. Owen, ed., *Deliberate Force: A Case Study in Effective Air Campaigning*, Maxwell AFB, AL: Air University Press, January 2000, on Bosnia 1995; and Benjamin S. Lambeth, *NATO's Air War for Kosovo: A Strategic and Operational Assessment*, Santa Monica, CA: RAND, 2001.

15. With thanks for the inspiration provided by Ian Kershaw: *Hitler, 1889-1936: Hubris*, London: Allen Lane, 1998; *Hitler, 1936-1943: Nemesis*, London: Allen Lane, 2000.

16. Robert H. Scales, Jr., *Certain Victory: The U.S. Army in the Gulf War*, Washington, DC: Office of the Chief of Staff, 1993; Norman Friedman, *Desert Victory: The War for Kuwait*, Annapolis, MD: Naval Institute Press, 1991. The Air Force story was told in Richard P. Hallion, *Storm over Iraq: Air Power and the Gulf War*, Washington, DC: Smithsonian Institution Press, 1992; and, in ways not wholly beloved by the USAF hierarchy, in its commissioned *Gulf War Air Power Survey* (GWAPS) (5 vols). See Thomas A. Keaney and Eliot A. Cohen, *Gulf War Air Power Survey, Summary Report*, Washington, DC: U.S. Government Printing Office, 1993. The official Air Force reaction to the GWAPS volumes was not notably dissimilar from the Royal Navy's distancing response to the volumes of the official history of Naval Operations in the Great War written by Julian S. Corbett.

17. For an influential British dissenting voice, see Michael Howard, "Mistake to Declare this is a 'War,'" *RUSI Journal,* Vol. 146, No. 6, December 2001, pp. 1-4.

18. Williamson Murray and Allan R. Millett, writing about 1940, have commented that "For the Germans, the victory over France suggested that everything was possible for the Third Reich." *A War to be Won: Fighting the Second World War*, Cambridge, MA: Harvard University Press, 2000, p. 89.

19. Lawrence Freedman, "The Third World War?" *Survival,* Vol. 43, No. 4, Winter 2001, pp. 61-88.

20. Save with reference to politically meaningless and morally abominable destructive potential, nuclear armaments almost certainly rendered the two superpowers less powerful than they would have been without the nuclear discovery. Today, nuclear arms are the weapons of the weak, not the strong. The U.S. Government in 2002 is thoroughly disinterested in its nuclear arsenal, save only for its uncertain residual value to help deter the threat or use of weapons of mass destruction against U.S. interests. Usable American military power is thoroughly conventional. The nuclear emphasis in recent Russian military doctrine attests to Moscow's appreciation of the weakness of its conventional forces.

21. Russell F. Weigley, *The Age of Battles: The Quest for Decisive Warfare from Breitenfeld to Waterloo*, Bloomington, IN: Indiana University Press, 1991, p. xiii.

22. *Ibid.*

23. For recent presentations of the realist paradigm, see Colin S. Gray, "Clausewitz Rules, OK? The Future is the Past—with GPS," in Michael Cox, Ken Booth, and Tim Dunne, eds., *The Interregnum: Controversies in World Politics, 1989-1999,* Cambridge: Cambridge University Press, 1999, pp. 161-182; and John J. Measheimer, *The Tragedy of Great Power Politics*, New York: W.W. Norton, 2001.

24. By far the most intelligent discussion of "the origins of great wars" is T. C. W. Blanning, *The Origins of the French Revolutionary Wars*, London: Longman, 1986, ch. 1. Recent studies include Stephen Van Evera, *Causes of War: Power and the Roots of Conflict*, Ithaca, NY: Cornell University Press, 1999; and Dale C. Copeland, *The Origins of Major War*, Ithaca, NY: Cornell University Press, 2000. It is surprising how many scholars fail to grasp both the vital distinction between the

causes of war and the causes of wars, and the need for theory to explain periods of peace as well as outbreaks of war.

25. Weigley, *Age of Battles,* p. 543.

26. Clausewitz, *On War,* p. 605.

27. See the innovative analysis in Stephen J. Cimbala, *Clausewitz and Chaos: Friction in War and Military Policy*, Westport, CT: Praeger Publishers, 2001.

28. See Michael Howard, "When are Wars Decisive?" *Survival,* Vol. 41, No. 1, Spring 1999, p. 129.

29. For a most insightful discussion of the relationship between the conduct of war and the securing of a tolerable peace, see Brian Bond, *The Pursuit of Victory: From Napoleon to Saddam Hussein*, Oxford: Oxford University Press, 1996.

30. Howard, "When are Wars Decisive?" p. 135.

31. Clausewitz, *On War,* p. 75.

32. "Few wars, in fact, are any longer decided on the battlefield, if indeed they ever were. They are decided at the peace table. Military victories do not themselves determine the outcome of wars; they only provide political opportunities for the victors—and even those opportunities are likely to be limited by circumstances beyond their control." Howard, "When are Wars Decisive?" p. 130. Howard comes close to overstating a persuasive point.

33. Readers tired of the literature that is largely dismissive of U.S. and ARVN military efforts could do worse than examine the evidence and arguments in Mark W. Woodruff, *Unheralded Victory: Who Won the Vietnam War?*, New York: Harper Collins, 1999; and C. Dale Walton, *The Myth of Inevitable U.S. Defeat in Vietnam*, London: Frank Cass, 2002. On the events of 1972, see Dale Andrade, *Trial by Fire: The 1972 Easter Offensive, America's Last Vietnam Battle*, New York: Hippocrene Books, 1995.

34. See Colin S. Gray, *Modern Strategy*, Oxford: Oxford University Press, 1999, ch. 1; and Richard K. Betts, "Is Strategy an Illusion?" *International Security*, Vol. 25, No. 2, Fall 2000, pp. 5-50.

35. Colin S. Gray, "Why Strategy Is Difficult," *Joint Force Quarterly,* No. 22, Summer 1999, pp. 6-12.

36. On the McNamara years, see Alain Enthoven and K. Wayne Smith, *How Much Is Enough? Shaping the Defense Program, 1961-1969*, New York: Harper and Row, 1971.

37. See Terence Zuber, "The Schlieffen Plan Reconsidered," *War in History,* Vol. 6, No. 3, July 1999, pp. 262-305; and Antulio J. Echevarria, II, *After Clausewitz: German Military Thinkers Before the Great War*, Lawrence, KS: University Press of Kansas, 2000, pp. 193-94.

38. Clausewitz, *On War,* pp. 75, 77.

39. Richard P. Henrick, *Crimson Tide*, New York: Avon Books, 1995, p. 75. I am grateful to Richard Betts for bringing this brilliant interpretation of Clausewitz to my notice.

40. Robert Endicott Osgood, *Limited War: The Challenge to American Strategy*, Chicago: University of Chicago Press, 1957, was probably the finest product of the civilian exploration of limited war.

41. Schelling, *Arms and Influence,* ch. 1.

42. See Stephen Peter Rosen, "Vietnam and the American Theory of Limited War," *International Security,* Vol. 7, No. 2, Fall 1982, pp. 83-113, for a hard hitting critique.

43. Clausewitz, *On War,* p. 605.

44. See Bernard Brodie, *Strategy in the Missile Age*, Princeton, NJ: Princeton University Press, 1959, pp. 21-27. The "principles" receive fair scholarly treatment in John I. Alger, *The Quest for Victory: The History of the Principles of War*, Westport, CT: Greenwood Press, 1982.

45. For the best of modern scholarship, see the different views in Martin van Creveld, *Supplying War: Logistics from Wallenstein to Patton*, Cambridge: Cambridge University Press, 1977; John A. Lynn, ed., *Feeding Mars: Logistics in Western Warfare from the Middle Ages to the Present*, Boulder, CO: Westview Press, 1993; and Thomas M. Kane, *Military Logistics and Strategic Performance*, London: Frank Cass, 2001.

46. Hew Strachan observes of the war in German East Africa, that "Both the climate . . . and the insect life. . . were strategically decisive." *The First World War: Vol. 1, To Arms*, Oxford: Oxford University Press, 2001, p. 504.

47. Recent examinations include Lawrence Freedman, ed., *Strategic Coercion: Concepts and Cases*, Oxford: Oxford University

Press, 1998; and Stephen J. Cimbala, *Coercive Military Strategy*, College Station, TX: Texas A & M University Press, 1998.

48. The strategic malady of "victory fever" is recognized appropriately in Paul S. Dull, *A Battle History of the Imperial Japanese Navy, 1941-1945*, Annapolis, MD: Naval Institute Press, 1978.

49. Clausewitz, *On War,* p. 607.

50. See Gray: *Modern Strategy,* pp. 19-23; and *Weapons for Strategic Effect: How Important is Technology?* Occasional Paper No. 21, Maxwell AFB, AL: Center for Strategy and Technology, Air War College, January 2001.

51. Victor Davis Hanson, *Why the West Has Won: Carnage and Culture from Solamis to Vietnam*, London: Faber and Faber, 2001, risks taking a powerful culturalist argument a step too far.

52. Jeremy Black, *War in the New Century*, London: Continuum, 2001, p. vii.

53. Hanson, *Why the West Has Won,* ch. 4.

54. The most comprehensive treatment to date is Horst Boog and others, *Germany and the Second World War: Vol. IV, The Attack on the Soviet Union*, Oxford: Clarendon Press, 1998.

55. Black, *War in the New Century,* p. vii. He argues that war's multiple contexts is fatal for the RMA thesis.

56. Quoted *ibid.*, p. 2.

57. For reasons none too hard to glean from Michael Burleigh, *The Third Reich: A New History*, London: Macmillan, 2000.

58. Clausewitz, *On War,* p. 85.

59. *Ibid.*, p. 86.

60. See J. P. Harris, *Amiéns to the Armistice: The BEF in the Hundred Days' Campaign, 8 August—11 November 1918*, London: Brassey's, 1998.

61. A proposition argued persuasively in Murray and Millett, *War to be Won,* p. 483.

62. See David G. Chandler, *The Campaigns of Napoleon*, London: Weidenfeld and Nicolson, 1967, Part 17. Napoleon's forte was the operational level of war. As an artilleryman granted command of the army of Italy in 1796, Napoleon—unlike Wellington—had no experience of leading infantry in battle. Napoleon's military genius was not tactical.

63. Antoine Henri de Jomini, *The Art of War*, 1838, Novato, CA: Presidio Press, 1992, p. 325.

64. *Ibid.*, p. 70

65. See Strachan, *First World War,* p. 724.

66. John Shy, "Jomini," in Peter Paret, ed., *Makers of Modern Strategy: from Machiavelli to the Nuclear Age*, Princeton, NJ: Princeton University Press, 1986, pp. 183-184.

67. Edward N. Luttwak, *Strategy: The Logic of War and Peace,* 2nd ed., Cambridge, MA: Harvard University Press, 2001.

68. Daniel Goure gushes as follows: "RMA advocates need fear no longer [that others might exploit the RMA first]. The RMA they predicted is here and the USA holds an unquestionable, perhaps even unchallengeable lead. The war in Afghanistan demonstrates the reality of the RMA and shows first how far the USA has come in owning and exploiting it." "Location, Location, Location," *Jane's Defence Weekly,* February 27, 2002.

69. J. F. C. Fuller, *Armament and History*, London: Eyre and Spottiswoode, 1946. For an outstanding recent discussion, see Eliot Cohen, "Technology and Warfare," in John Baylis and others, eds., *Strategy in the Contemporary World: An Introduction to Strategic Studies*, Oxford: Oxford University Press, 2002, pp. 235-253.

70. Norman Friedman, *The Fifty-Year War: Conflict and Strategy in the Cold War*, Annapolis, MD: Naval Institute Press, 2000, Part 6, tells a plausible tale, keyed to Soviet unreadiness to meet the computer age.

71. See Andrew F. Krepinevich, Jr., *The Army and Vietnam*, Baltimore: Johns Hopkins University Press, 1986, esp. pp. 112-127, 168-172; and Shelby Stanton, *The 1st Cav in Vietnam: Anatomy of a Division*, Novato, CA: Presidio Press, 1999.

72. For Russian perspectives on their Afghan experience, see Lester W. Grau, ed., *The Bear Went over the Mountain: Soviet Combat Tactics in Afghanistan*, London: Frank Cass, 1998. For Afghan perspectives it

would be difficult to better Mohammad Yousaf and Mark Adkin, *Afghanistan—The Bear Trap: The Defeat of a Superpower*, Barnsley, UK: Leo Cooper, 2001, esp. ch. 11, "Wonder Weapons—Gunships versus Stingers."

73. Alfred Thayer Mahan, *The Influence of Sea Power upon the French Revolution and Empire, 1793-1812*, Vol. 1, Boston: Little Brown, 1898, p. 102. I thank Jon Sumida for bringing this Mahanian dictum to my attention.

74. Hanson, *Why the West Has Won,* p. 360.

75. Cohen, "Technology and Warfare," pp. 247-248.

76. The question of substitution of strength for weakness among strategy's dimensions is central to the argument in Colin S. Gray, *Strategy for Chaos: RMA Theory and the Evidence of History*, London: Frank Cass, 2002.

77. Colin S. Gray, "Thinking Asymmetrically in Times of Terror," *Parameters,* Vol. 32, No. 1, Spring 2002, pp. 5-14.

78. For a terse persuasive statement of America's contemporary role, see Donald Kagan, *On the Origins of War and the Preservation of Peace*, New York: Doubleday, 1995, pp. 566-573.

79. As Eliot Cohen has noted, the military and strategic effectiveness of America's information-led RMA cannot be assessed properly until it is tested in combat against much more worthy foes than have been trounced thus far. "Technology and Warfare," p. 243.

80. Many countries, though militarily grossly inferior to the United States, still could pose dangerous challenges through investment in "niche" capabilities which could stress U.S. defenses and values. Expertise relevant to information warfare is globally distributed, and the entry price is financially modest. A large balanced blue-water fleet is nice to have, but a handful of super-quiet diesel submarines and a large and well-dispersed inventory of ballistic and cruise missiles, particularly if assisted by some aerial or space based targeting aids, which admittedly would be very difficult to employ, could cause Americans acute anxieties. Should some missiles be loaded with WMD, in part to compensate for targeting uncertainties, the U.S. military could find itself committed to a whole new world of pain. There is much merit in Robert H. Scales, Jr., "Adaptive Enemies: Dealing with the Strategic Threat After 2010," *Strategic Review,* Vol. 27, No. 1, Winter 1999, pp. 5-14.

81. Robert M. Utley, *Cavalier in Buckskin: George Armstrong Custer and the Western Military Frontier*, Norman, OK: University of Oklahoma Press, 1988, p. 206.

> Custer never thought like an Indian. With most of his peers, therefore, he was doomed to fight Indians with the techniques of conventional warfare. For a century the army fought Indians as if they were British or Mexicans or Confederates. Each Indian war was expected to be the last, and so the generals never developed a doctrine or organization adapted to the special problems posed by the Indian style of fighting.

Also see Sam C. Sarkesian, *America's Forgotten Wars: The Counterrevolutionary Past and Lessons for the Future*, Westport, CT: Greenwood Press, 1984, which is a neglected minor classic.

82. Charles E. Heller and William A. Stofft, eds., *America's First Battles, 1776-1965*, Lawrence, KS: University Press of Kansas, 1986, is valuable.

83. The classic text is Charles A. Callwell, *Small Wars: A Tactical Textbook for Imperial Soldiers*, 1906 ed.; Novato, CA: Presidio Press, 1990.

84. See John Haldon, *Warfare, State and Society in the Byzantine World, 565-1204*, London: UCL Press, 1999, ch. 2.

8

5. See Edward Spiers, "The Late Victorian Army, 1868-1914," in David Chandler and Ian Beckett, eds., *The Oxford Illustrated History of the British Army*, Oxford: Oxford University Press, 1994, pp. 189-214; T. R. Moreman, *The Army in India and the Development of Frontier Warfare, 1889-1947*, London: Macmillan, 1998; and John Gooch, ed., *The Boer War: Direction, Experience and Image*, London: Frank Cass, 2000.

86. At least if modern scholars are to be believed. See Adrian Keith Goldsworthy, *The Roman Army at War, 100 BC—AD 200*, Oxford: Oxford University Press, 1996, ch. 3.

87. Sun-tzu, *The Art of War,* Ralph D. Sawyer, trans., Boulder, CO: Westview Press, 1994, p. 179.

88. There is much to recommend this thought of Ralph Peters: "In this age of technological miracles, our military needs to study mankind." *Fighting for the Future: Will America Triumph?* Mechanicsburg, PA: Stackpole Books, 1999, p. 172.

89. See Keith B. Payne, *The Fallacies of Cold War Deterrence and a New Direction*, Lexington, KY: University Press of Kentucky, 2001.

90. See, for example, Philip Smucker, "Blunders that let bin Laden slip away," *The Daily Telegraph*, London, February 23, 2002, p. 20.

91. On the logic of international competition, see John J. Mearsheimer, *The Tragedy of Great Power Politics*, New York: W. W. Norton, 2001.

92. Robert Allan Doughty, *The Breaking Point: Sedan and the Fall of France, 1940*, Hamden, CT: Archon Books, 1990, tells the story of tactical and operational disaster well.

93. See David M. Glantz and Jonathan House, *When Titans Clashed: How the Red Army Stopped Hitler*, Lawrence, KS: University Press of Kansas, 1995.

94. The main title tells all in Qiao Liang and Wan Xiangsui, *Unrestricted Warfare: Assumptions on War and Tactics in the Age of Globalization*, Beijing: PLA Literature Arts Publishing House, February 1999. China could well prove to be a dangerous, asymmetrical opponent, one compelled to think imaginatively by America's regular military strengths.

95. See Victor Davis Hanson, *The Western Way of War: Infantry Battle in Classical Greece*, London: Hodder and Stoughton, 1989; and Stephen Mitchell, "Hoplite Warfare in Ancient Greece," in Alan B. Lloyd, ed., *Battle in Antiquity*, London: Gerald Duckworth, 1996, pp. 87-105.

96. Mao Tse-tung, attrib., *On Guerrilla Warfare,* Samuel B. Griffith, trans., New York: Frederick A. Praeger, 1961, p. 52.

97. See Michael I. Handel, *Masters of War: Classical Strategic Thought,* 3rd ed., London: Frank Cass, 2001, Appendix B: "The Weinberger Doctrine."